A 90-DAY JOURNEY

JIM BRANDENBURG CHASED BY THE LIGHT

NORTHWORD PRESS

At an East Texas lunch counter, I got into a discussion with the man sitting next to me about wildlife photography. The man said, "Oh, yeah. Jim Brandenburg. He's the wolf guy isn't he?" "Well, sort of," I replied. Wolf guy? Other descriptions came to mind: Naturalist, landscape photographer, wildlife champion. How about calling him a visionary who produces heartfelt, thought-provoking work? True, but still far short of the whole truth. ✍ Jim's work brings us the natural world in portraits of light and shadow. We see blades of grass silver with frost, golden shafts of light, verdant sweeps of trees as well as the realities of life and death in nature. He does not capture nature; rather his work tells a love story, a mutual seduction, for both are courted and both are suitor. ✍ On one assignment he journeyed thousands of miles to find images of the North American landscape as it might have existed before the arrival of Europeans. In this new project, he often traveled only steps out his back door near Ely, Minnesota, yet discovered compelling images of transcendent beauty.

✍ Having known and worked with Jim over the decades, I expected to be delighted with the work, but wasn't prepared for the surprise I received from only three rolls of film out of the Minnesota North Woods. Many assignments now burn a thousand rolls or more to produce the twenty or so images we use in an article for *National Geographic* magazine. ✍ One of our illustration editors, John Echave, visited Jim for a previous assignment and was the first to see this project. John recognized the worth of the ninety photographs from Jim's three-month self-assignment and asked if he could show them to me. As we reviewed the photos, it took only the first few frames for me to realize the magnitude of what Jim had done. I knew we were seeing a remarkable project, and I immediately wanted to publish it in our magazine. ✍ Self-assigned project. Sounds simple enough. Pick something you like and shoot it. Explore a place. Support a cause. Work when you can. It's over when you say it's over. Not much pressure. Frequently young photographers will pursue a self—assignment to prove themselves, to lift spirits when rejections pile up, to impress an editor, or to awaken inspiration when assignment work becomes oppressive. ✎ But what if you are one of the finest photographers in the world? You have no need to build a portfolio or impress anyone. No need to challenge your skill each day for ninety days—especially if you have no real intention of publishing the photographs. Why restrict yourself to exposing one frame a day? Why such pressure? ✎ Jim answers these questions in the following pages as he displays the vision, discipline, and drive that marks him as an exceptional talent. ✎ Self-assigned projects may begin with the head—to satisfy an intellectual curiosity—however, more often the heart leads. ✎ For a normal *National Geographic* story the senior editors discuss a proposal submitted by a writer, photographer, scientist, or staff member with two questions in mind: Will it enlighten readers? Is it intellectually, emotionally, and visually worthy of the investment of months or years of peoples'

lives to produce it? ✎ Sometimes, the photographs answer both questions at first sight. ✎ Rarely have I seen a set of photographs like these which lead to new discoveries with each viewing. With every frame we see the breadth of nature in a single shot. For me the perfection of each image is heightened by understanding the discipline and drive required to maintain the vision through the three months. A tour-de-force. ✎ Jim's three—month journey began as an exer—cise in the fundamentals of nature photography: focus, light, study. In the end, it came to mean much more. ✎ Knowing the trials Jim endured to produce the photographs, I hesitate to mention this, but I can't help wonder what the other nine months of the year might reveal.

—William Allen
Editor, *National Geographic* magazine

In a dark spruce forest—two lakes and a portage from my remote bush camp—I have discovered a place of mystery and wonder. In these quiet woods I sense the primeval, an impression that no one has stood there before. So it seemed natural that this is where I would go on the first day of my photographic journey. 🪶 I had set myself a challenge: that for ninety days between the autumnal equinox and winter solstice I would make only one photograph a day. There would be no second exposure, no second chance. My work would be stripped to the bones, bringing together whatever photographic and woods skills I have. 🪶 My quest was both arbitrary and rigid. Arbitrary in that no one had compelled me, or even asked me, to perform it. Rigid in that, once engaged, the constraints I had chosen would force me to examine myself, my art, and the wild and isolated place in which I live in a manner I'd never before attempted. 🪶 Knowing that success would depend not upon any single and magnificent image but rather upon a tapestry woven of furtive glances, I arose before dawn that first morning, anxious to begin at that place where I felt nature kept some of her hidden secrets. A cool mist rose and licked my face as I paddled across the two small lakes. The forest was dead quiet as I stalked through somber bogs.

While the day smelled of dawn, I reached my secret spot, a cragged forest the likes of which can still be found stretching unbroken to far-off Hudson Bay.   Perhaps because that spruce forest is not so overtly beautiful—no vistas, no magnificent trees, no coursing waterways—it has remained untrampled. And perhaps that is why I have always felt that something spiritual lived there, something slightly dark and old.   Green pillows of ankle-deep moss rise above the forest floor. Bent grasses hint at the passing of unseen winds and spirits. Spires of black spruce, limbless to beyond the height of a moose, rise out of the moss and point toward the sky, their broken branches draped with a haunting, thin gauze of lichens. Deadly red-capped mushrooms stand like miniature tables and chairs, fungus furniture that might have served the little people that are so much a part of the folklore of the native Ojibwe and my own Norwegian ancestors.   I passed by some tempting photographs that first morning—a row of five juvenile grouse sitting at attention on a diagonal log, some energetic Canada jays willing to comically pose—to make a photograph of moss, mushrooms, and trees. And although the subjects could not move, as I set up my tripod and framed the scene, I was conscious that no matter how earthbound the substance was, its essence was fleeting, and would be as elusive to capture as the image of a white wolf in a snowfall.

9:15 am   Black spruce forest

9:15 am 🖋 Black spruce forest

2:50 pm ✿ Jack pine on lake shore

6:50 pm ✿ Evening primrose

8:30 am Turkey vulture

5:15 pm 🐝 Raven feather in rain

2:10 pm Ruffed grouse

There would be but a single chance to collect it. My shutter opened, then closed. My journey began. Like Thoreau,

who had gone to the woods because he "wished to live deliberately, to front only essential facts of life" and to "transact some pri-

vate business with the fewest obstacles," I embraced this endeavor, with some trepidation, to see if I could find what had drawn

me so long ago to my art, and to see if I had become as perceptive of nature as I hoped. "To anticipate, not the sunrise and the

dawn merely, but, if possible, Nature herself," wrote Thoreau. Nature cannot be twisted to our whims, not even for the

purpose of capturing her beauty on film. She must be approached on a level at once aware of both her charms and her harshness.

Hers is not a world solely of "calendar" scenes—of which I've shot many and would, alas, shoot more of over the ninety days—

but one also of mystery and hardness, built of the timeless recycling of energy as creatures and plants die and are reborn.

Thoreau's "sunrise" is the calendar photograph that comprises what for some is their sole understanding of nature. My hope was

that I would be able to cajole from her something deeper. The success or failure of my effort is here for you to see and judge.

2:00 pm ✎ Cedar grove – US/Canada border

2:00 pm Cedar grove – US/Canada border

3:55 pm   Ruffed grouse on moss

OCTOBER

S A T U R D A Y **1**

7:15 am Common mergansers

This has been an immensely personal project—when originally conceived I had no intention of publishing the results, and I feel somewhat vulnerable in sharing it. I saw it rather as a process. Through my studies in Japan, I have been moved by how the traditional Japanese honor a place through a self-suffering focus or intensity. Like an ascetic Buddhist monk who sits hourly in contemplation, hoping that a sacrifice of nonessentials will lead to some higher level, I was intrigued by the idea that through such a Zen-like approach I might be led to scenes that defined not only my relationship to nature, but to the essence of my home, the boreal forest. Such a process would be meaningful to me. As is honoring nature. I was also feeling increasing dissatisfaction with my photography. Today's technology has made photography somewhat easier, and I found that I had grown as reliant upon—or trapped by—that technology as anyone. The sheer number of photographs taken was also overwhelming. On an average three-month assignment for *National Geographic* I might use up to 300 rolls; 1,000 rolls is often not unusual for some photographers. At 36 frames per roll, that would mean 36,000 exposures would be made for a 30-page feature. What had become of the process and profession I had so dearly loved?

S U N **2** D A Y

7:10 am   Boundary Waters loons

7:10 am · Boundary Waters loons

6:30 pm ❦ Fallen black spruce melts into bog

6:50 pm ❦ Shovel Point – Lake Superior

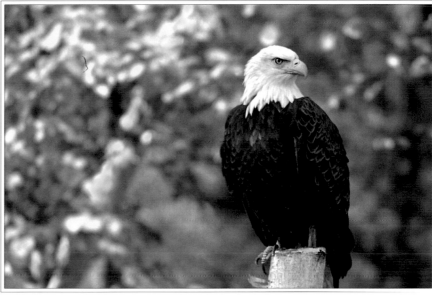

2:55 pm 🐝 Great blue heron

9:45 am 🐝 Bald eagle

My photography had originally been a means, and an excuse, for spending time out-of-doors, but in the midst of my own success I found myself wed to a drudge named technology, living in a world lit by computer screens instead of the sun. I wanted to wander the forest, to see what was over the next rise, to follow animal tracks in the snow as I had done so happily as a boy. Each photograph would be a true original, like a painting. Not the best selected from rolls and rolls of similar frames, and not altered in any manner except occasional cropping or adjusting tone and color. I sensed there would be new lessons learned.

There were, but not always those that I had imagined. Some were merely lessons remembered, recapturing things I had forgotten, such as remaining open to chance, and that, in nature, not all beauty is giant in scale. One such lesson occurred on October 15th, the twenty-third day. It was late and I despaired of capturing anything of value. The day was dark and gloomy; my mood reflected the weather. I wandered through the dripping forest all day long. Tired, hungry, and wet, I was near tears. I was mentally beating myself for having passed up several deer portraits and the chance to photograph a playful otter. None of those scenes spoke to me at the time.

4:30 pm 🐝 Paper birch grove

OCTOBER

FRIDAY 17

4:30 pm · Paper birch grove

4:50 pm ❧ Norway pines at Wolf Ridge   7:45 am ❧ Raven Lake with Lake Superior

6:30 pm 🌸 Sunset

5:10 pm 🐝 Rose hips

6:30 pm ❧ Norway pine bark

5:40 pm 🌿 On my path to the lake   2:30 pm 🌿 Black ducks and mallards

But perhaps because I was patient, and perhaps because, as natives do on a vision quest, I had reached my physical limits, I became open to the possibility revealed by a single red maple leaf floating on a dark-water pond.　　My spirits rose the instant I saw it, and although the day was very late and what little light there had been was fleeing rapidly, I studied the scene from every angle. Finally, unsure of my choice, I made the shot anyway, thankful at least that the long day had ended.　　Once more I was surprised by the result. The image seems to have a lyrical quality, with a rhythm in the long grass. A brooding sky reflects back on the water. Although when I had first framed it in the viewfinder it was quite disappointing, on film it gave me happy sur-prise. I know that what I see isn't what you will see—for me, this photograph is a lesson in diligence and patience. It speaks to me of intimacy as well, reminds me to look closely at the world. As in life, you never really know what it is you have until later, upon reflection.　　Another lesson occurred on October 17th, day twenty-five. Although I had tried to devote my full attention to this project, business and life itself kept intruding. On this day, I was forced to find a subject without the luxury of allowing the proper time to lead me to it.

S A T U **15** R D A Y

6:05 pm ☙ Maple leaf in pond

6:05 pm ✓ *Maple leaf in pond*

OCTOBER

S U N **16** D A Y

12:30 pm Heavy rain in the boreal forest

Walking to a granite ridge not far from home, I searched for a scene "worthy" of my one photograph. I was tense, and not just a little irritable. And then a breeze blew. If you have been in a paper birch forest far from roads and human noise, you know then that tatters of birch bark rattle in the breeze like parchment scrolls clattering to the floor. Hearing that sound, I turned to a tree right next to me. Torn and hanging from it was a sheet of chalky white bark, revealing its apricot-colored underlayer.

Constrained by time, I "settled" for this subject, composing the shot and tripping the shutter rather in haste. But when I later viewed the printed image, I was pleased to be reminded of something that I had long ago learned. Like Japanese haiku poetry, sometimes more is less; and in nature, beauty or meaning need not be on a large scale. I had returned to the roots of my photography. If some of the scenes asked me to turn inward, many demanded that I look outward, to embrace nature viscerally, even to participate. While I wandered through the woodland, the land's wild residents struggled daily. You will see a picture of a dead doe's lost gaze. After a rude, piercing midnight gunshot, the dawn's fussing of ravens and eagles led me to the scene of the crime. A deer had been wantonly killed by a poacher.

4:30 pm ☙ Paper birch

OCTOBER

MONDAY 17

4:30 pm 🖊 Paper birch

41

3:59 pm 🐾 Discovery Lake   5:47 pm 🐾 White-tailed deer skull

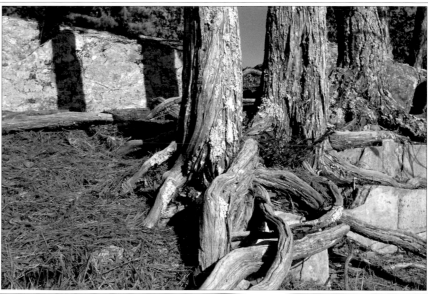

12:25 pm   White–tailed doe and fawn   10:24 am   Island cedars

1:22 pm Willows and rain

6:33 pm 🦋 Lichen rock

4:31 pm 🦋 Quiet pond

5:11 pm ❧ Reindeer moss

8:09 am ❧ Killing frost

5:24 pm 🐾 Life on a ledge

6:17 pm 🐾 Ravenwood Falls

6:00 pm ☙ Wilderness sunset

4:04 am Aurora borealis

8:04 am Judd Lake

NOVEMBER

T U E S **1** D A Y

7:42 am   Frosty sedge meadow

3:15 pm 🌿 Hairy woodpecker

2:26 pm 🐝 Mink at Judd Lake

4:41 pm 🦢 Boundary Waters dusk

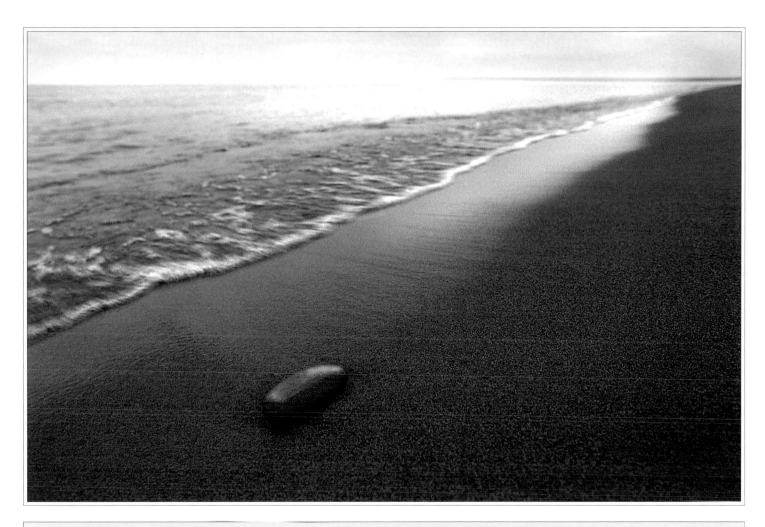

4:22 pm   Lake Superior beach

2:23 pm ❧ Black-backed woodpecker

3:58 pm ❧ Beaver cuttings on birch

3:26 pm   Red squirrel

12:12 pm   Ice by stream

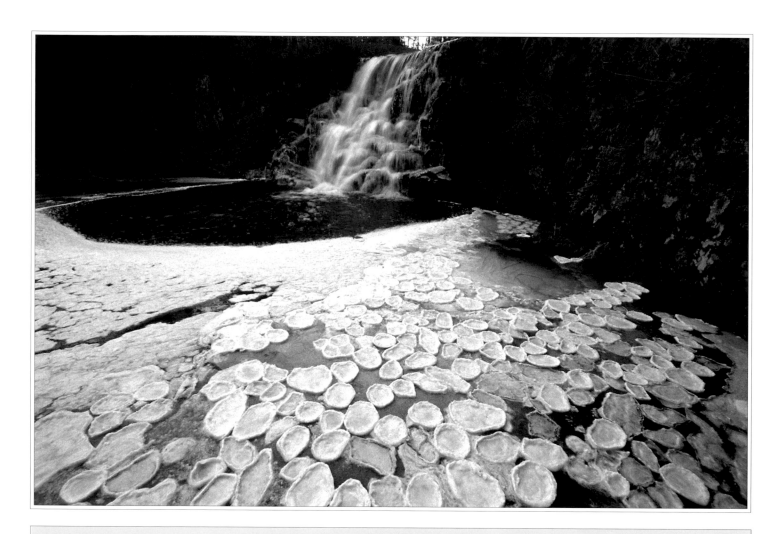

8:22 am 🦋 Pancake ice at Ravenwood Falls

4:22 pm ❦ Nuthatch tail

3:57 pm ❦ Lichen-covered cliff with quartz

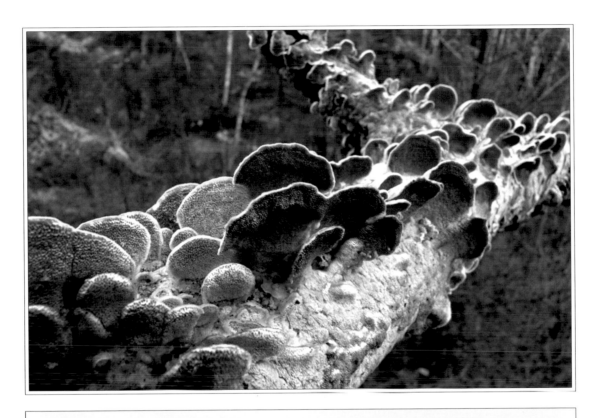

3:58 pm 🍄 350-year-old cedars   2:32 pm 🍄 Bracket fungus on branch

10:58 am 🐚 Pond ice

3:43 pm   Fallen leaf

3:36 pm   Lichens on ancient bedrock

You will see yet another lifeless deer, part of a more respectable ancient drama, this one brought down by wolves. This I also witnessed by sound and arrived while the body was just opened and still steaming in the below-zero air. This, I might argue, is the more natural and pardonable "crime." There is the photograph of a loon dancing at sunrise, a loon I had only moments before caught from my canoe so that I might remove an embedded fish hook and line that had become entangled about its neck and bill. This image provokes an especially fond memory. Otherwise doomed to a cruel and certain death, this young loon swam off with its nervous and protective parent, then stopped and gratefully flapped its wings as if to say thank you. All around me I witnessed the cycle of life and death—with deer becoming wolves, bones becoming soil, lichens eating rocks, herons stalking fish. Irate wolves chased ravens, who in turn teased indifferent eagles, while I wandered in the knowledge that my quiet contemplation would lead me to them so that I might paint them on film. These experiences rekindled in me a deep primordial feeling, perhaps the same feelings an ancient hunter had once had. There was the very real "thrill of the hunt," buried emotions that I first experienced as a boy tracking foxes across the snow-covered prairie where I was raised.

9:25 am Poacher–killed deer

9:25 am 🦌 Poacher-killed deer

1:52 pm ❦ Abandoned beaver dam

9:48 am ❦ Bubbles under ice

1:58 pm ❧ White spruce in snowfall

3:14 pm ❧ Bad weather—Burntside Lake

8:06 am Border Lake — below zero

8:14 am   Wolf and fox tracks on new ice

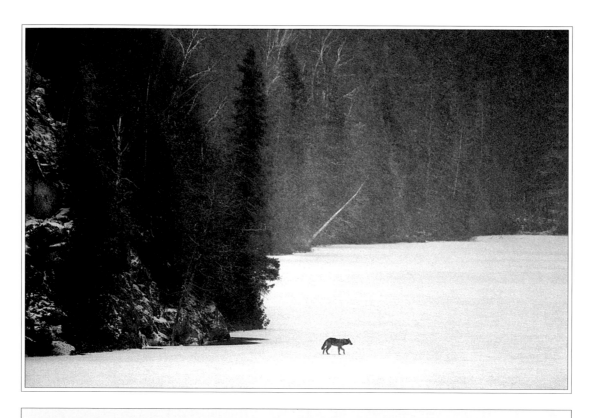

8:52 am 🌿 Timber wolf testing lake ice   8:02 am 🌿 Timber wolf eating deer

Some of the photographs that resulted from these experiences—chance encounters with wolves, white-tailed deer, quick mink on shorelines—would not have been published had I been my usual self-critic. They are noteworthy to me nonetheless in that I somehow was led at the right instant to the spot where these animals presented themselves to me, and was able to record that moment with one exposure. The excitement surrounding those moments was palpable. All my woods skills of stalking and reading sign came into play, and like those of our ancestors poised with a spear or bow, my body tensed. In the end, this project changed me. I feel memory aftershock now when I revisit the scenes where these photographs were made. The emotions experienced at that instant of the shutter's click well up anew inside me. The project altered my view of photography as well, for routine photography today seems rather tedious by comparison, which, I guess, should come as no surprise. It was partially a dissatisfaction with the act of "ordinary" photography that had brought me to this task. This ritual and simple study reminded me of what I had forgotten, and took on overtones of prayer and homage. This is my lost mythology that celebrates life, marks a passage in my career, and honors the cycle of nature that surrounds me in this northern forest. "Mythology helps you to identify the mysteries of the energies pouring through you. Therein lies your eternity." *Joseph Campbell*

NOVEMBER

S U N 2 7 D A Y

8:14 am   Wolf following shoreline

NOVEMBER

SUNDAY 27

8:14 am ☞ Wolf following shoreline

2:05 pm   Ravens and eagle at Judd Lake   12:10 pm   Ravens teasing eagle

11:29 am   Red fox tracks on Lake One

DECEMBER

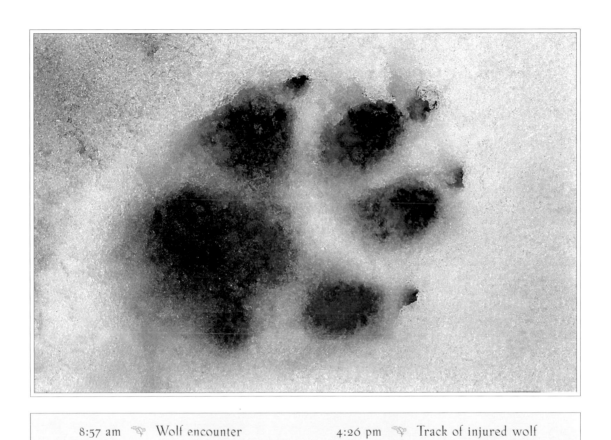

8:57 am   🐾   Wolf encounter   4:26 pm   🐾   Track of injured wolf

1:48 pm ❧ Frozen Ravenwood Falls

3:04 pm ❧ Looking toward the wilderness

12:34 pm ❧ Long shadows

11:38 am ❧ Moose Lake shoreline

3:05 pm ❧ Discovery Lake

3:54 pm 🐝 Snowfall in the valley

F R I **9** D A Y

8:40 am   Wolf chasing ravens

11:13 am 🐝 Norway pine grove

8:20 am 🐝 Coyote and ravens

2:38 pm 🌱 Pine grosbeaks

10:43 am 🌱 Tree with bear markings

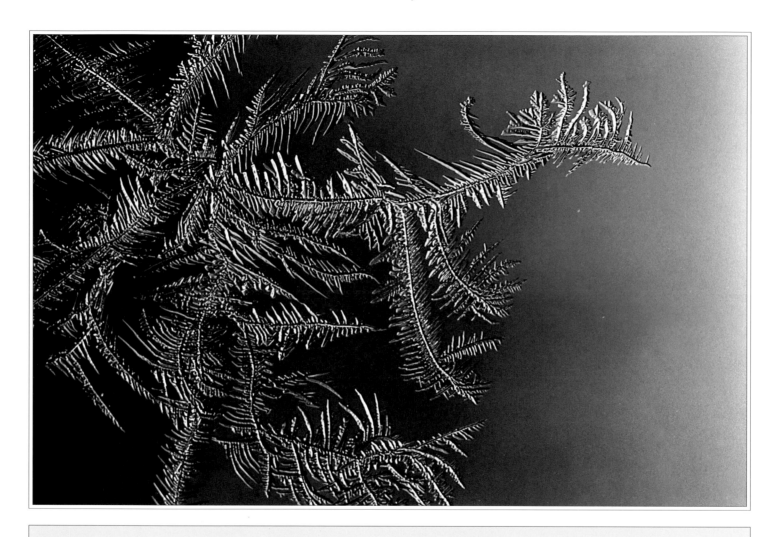

12:55 pm ❀ Frost on glass, bush camp

4:22 pm ❧ Patterns of branches   4:48 pm ❧ Cedar skeleton

2:02 pm 🐺 Wolf-killed deer

12:34 pm   Gray jay caching food for winter

7:15 am Full moon

The last two photographs—the sun hovering at low noon on the year's shortest day, and the moonlit forest just after midnight during the longest night—happened at winter solstice. They mark the end of my project and an ancient measure of a span of time. Since cryptic monoliths like Stonehenge were erected, we have sought to chronicle time and bottle its mystery. I chose this old division of time—this third season marking autumn and early winter—because of its power. Fruits of flesh and fiber have matured in the summer's warmth, after which this wild forest cools and grows darker. Life in the north grows tenuous, dramatic, even melancholy. Like my animal neighbors, I struggled with the pace of those ever-quickening days. More often than not I ended up capturing the day's image under its waning light. According to old Norse myths, the sun was always in a hurry, chased across the sky by a wolf named Skoll, who eventually will capture her. So too the moon is pursued by a wolf named Hati, who will devour him at the end of time. Thus time is hurried along by the wolves at its heels. For one who has spent so much of his life pursuing wolves, it is perhaps ironic that they, by chasing time, now pursued me, spurring me toward my goal.

DECEMBER

T U E 2 S O D A Y

12:00 pm ❧ Noon on year's shortest day

12:00 pm ✻ Noon on year's shortest day

1:40 am Year's longest night by moonlight

And although I use modern tools, I feel my work is kindred to that of the ancient artists who, amid the fumes and flames of tallow torches, created the animal tapestries that are the Lascaux cave paintings. No one will ever know why they composed those marvelous scenes, but I suspect that in an effort to survive nature, these ancient people knew they must become one with her, with the animals, as an expression of a "sympathetic magic." Try as we may, there is no analysis that can go beyond that—we simply are a part of nature and our soul always seeks that core. Our psyche has changed little over the ages. My ancestors, chased by hunger and the voracious cave bear, survived to celebrate with delicate imagery etched on their cold and dark living room walls. Today, I respectfully replay that same dance while being chased only by the light of a swift and hungry day.

ACKNOWLEDGMENTS

Even though the essence of this project appears to be very personal and solo in nature, the final result or even the ultimate success of this journey was linked in various and important ways to these dedicated individuals. For their help and support I am forever grateful.

Michael Furtman, who, when organization and even words failed me, came forward with his tremendous writing skills by giving a voice and clarity to my thoughts.

ProColor, Minneapolis, for their generous contribution in verifying the one–photograph–a–day process by processing and scanning the film with thoughtfulness and quality.

William Allen, who humbled me first by agreeing as editor to boldly publish this story in *National Geographic* magazine and second by writing his kind and thoughtful foreword in the front of this book.

Bill Arthur, a steady friend with a bright light for the path.

John Echave, for taking this unlikely project back to the *Geographic* and, with uncommon care, guiding it through the maze to the November 1997 issue.

Satoko Nakahara, for traveling from far abroad and sharing her extensive Japanese Zen sensitivities with me on the cherished trails of my north woods temple during this project. *Aibetsu-riku wa yo-no-narai*

Michio Hoshino, who was my stellar example of a nature photographer. Michio made his last trip back to nature in 1996 documenting the great bears he so honored. He is deeply missed. *Bansotsu wa eyasuku, isshō wa egatashi*

David Salmela, a gifted and caring architect, who not only shaped my beloved new forest home and studio during these 90 days, but buoyantly helped shape my frame of mind as well.

Anthony Brandenburg and Andy Baugnet for keeping the Minneapolis half of Ravenwood Studios alive and running during my 90-day absence.

Judy Brandenburg, my wife and confidant, who is not only the rudder and keel, but also the glue that holds this ship together and keeps it sailing in the right direction.

To that embattled and beguiling Boundary Waters Canoe Area Wilderness.

May it endure the meddling of man.

NorthWord Press, 5900 Green Oak Drive,
Minnetonka, MN 55343, 1-800-328-3895

For original photographic prints and expanded field day notes from this project
please contact:
Ravenwood Studios, 14568 Moose Lake Road, Ely, MN 55731, 218-365-5105
or visit us on the web at:

www.jimbrandenburg.com

ISBN 1-55971-671-1

First Edition

04 03 02 01 00 99 / 5 4 3